Chinese Bird-and-Flower Painting for Beginners

Ma Zhifeng

Translated by Wen Jingen with Pauline Cherrett

FOREIGN LANGUAGES PRESS

First Edition 2007

Text by Ma Zhifeng
English translation by Wen Jingen with Pauline Cherrett
Designed by Cai Rong
Art by Ma Zhifeng, Sun Shuming and Wen Jingen

Chinese Bird-and-Flower Painting for Beginners

ISBN 978-7-119-04812-3
© 2007 by Foreign Languages Press
Published by Foreign Languages Press
24 Baiwanzhuang Road, Beijing, 100037, China
Home page: http://www.flp.com.cn
Email address: info@flp.com.cn
sales@flp.com.cn
Distributed by China International Book Trading Corporation
35 Chegongzhuang Xilu, Beijing 100044, China
P. O. Box 399, Beijing, China

Printed in the People's Republic of China

Contents

Translator's notes:

1. All illustrations in this book were executed and provided by the author unless otherwise stated. 书中未注明作者的图片均为本书作者所作。

2. To make this book more accessible for non-Chinese readers, the translator has extensively edited the original text, and added some illustrations. The translator, and not the author, is responsible for all errors accruing from the rewriting and rearrangement.

为适应外国读者需要，本书编译过程中对原作的图文做了一定改动。着粪续貂，在所难免；所生舛误，咎在译者。敬希作者及读者见谅。

The greatest contribution the Chinese arts have made to the world is its bird-and-flower painting.

> *— Xu Beihong (Benteng Chi Fu Jian, [Galloping on a Foot-long Picture], Tianjin, Baihua wenyi chubanshe [Hundred-flower literary and art press], 2000, p. 252)*

Introduction

Wen Jingen and Pauline Cherrett

Birds and flowers are universally loved motifs, in China as well as in the West. Western artists show flowers in their works too, but as far as we know, Western artists seldom treat the bird-and-flower as a special genre, while in China it is a long-standing tradition.

Parrot, tinted etching

Western artists depict birds and flowers too

If an artist has an interest in this genre, it is natural for him or her to learn skills to paint birds and flowers, but if he or she does not mean to become a bird-and-flower painter, is there any point in learning bird-and-flower painting skills? The answer is affirmative.

Pair of cockerels by Pauline Cherrett (UK, b. 1946)

Beautiful Form before Faithful Form

An artist strives to produce forms that are both beautiful and faithful to life, but such forms are not always achievable. "Being true to life" is not a guarantee for a beautiful form. "Faithful" is not always beautiful, nor is "beautiful" always faithful. A faithful form looks exactly like a depicted human or object in nature while a beautiful form is one that conforms to certain aesthetic principles.

Multi-corolla Peach Blossom, sketch in pencil by Wen Jingen

This sketch from life is faithful but the branches forming the shape of a cross look awkward.

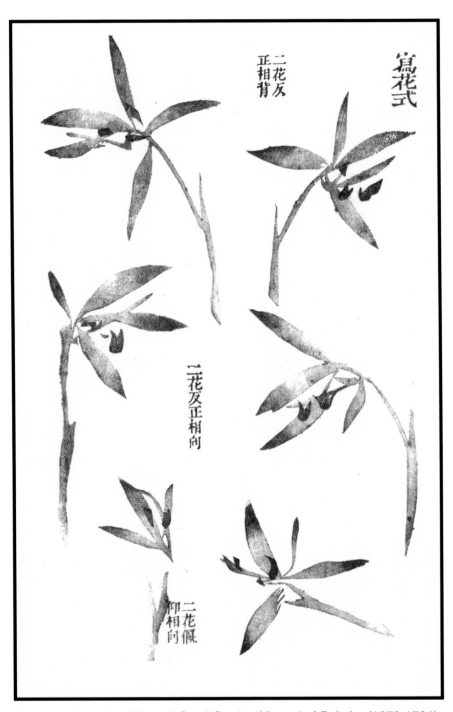

This page from the *Mustard Seed Garden Manual of Painting* (1679-1701) displays ways to produce beautiful forms of an orchid flower.

During 1950s and 1960s in China, "formalism" in arts was denounced by artists who embraced a creed of Socialist Realism. Drawing and painting from life was emphasised and copying ancient works took a back seat. Some artists believed that for a successful portrayal accurate forms were enough. But aesthetic principles governing beautiful forms do exist. Formal beauty is always an objective of artistic activities. The Chinese art historian Zhang Yanyuan in his *Lidai Minghua Ji* (*Records of Paintings through Dynasties*, AD 847) characterises early immature landscape paintings thus: "The mountain peaks...are arranged in the shapes of extending arms or fingers." (群峰……列植之状，则若伸臂布指。) The *Mustard Seed Garden Manual of Painting* (1679-1701) includes a formula concerning painting an orchid flower: "...the five petals (of an orchid flower) should not look like a flat palm, but they should be like fingers — some extending and others bending." These demonstrate that ancient Chinese artists came to realise a principle concerning beautiful forms: almost-parallel straight lines are undesirable. A truthful picture of an orchid flower may indeed have straight petals like the flat shape of a palm of the hand. Obviously, Chinese artists do not avoid such an image because it is unfaithful to life, they avoid it because it is not beautiful.

Chinese artists have summed up their experiences and boiled them down into formulae that best exhibit their aesthetic principles. It is Chinese bird-and-flower painting that contains the most of the depictive concepts.

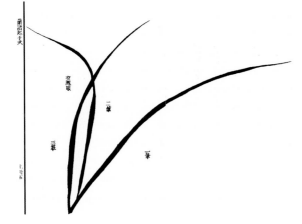

A page from the Mustard Seed Garden Manual of Painting (1679-1701)

This page shows the way to arrange leaves of an orchid. Once you learn this method, you will be able to make beautiful forms of other plants like lily and iris, too.

By copying methods of painting from textbooks, students will master some approaches to beautiful forms without delving into abstruse theories. Once an artist intuitively grasps these principles, he or she will be able to apply them to other genres of painting. That is the point of learning bird-and-flower — an artist learns to produce beautiful forms before he or she tries to portray the real world. In fact, a similar education system exists in the West too. In Victorian art schools, students were taught to draw objects that they could hardly have seen.

At the Source of the Peach Blossom Stream (detail) by Wen Zhengming (1470-1559)

The three trees on the foreground in this landscape are grouped in the same way as for orchid leaves — one long, the second short and the third crossing the other one or two.

Along with the arrangement of compositional elements, brushwork and ink application are very important factors in Chinese painting. To some extent they have their individual expressiveness. Chinese artists do not only produce lines and apply colours with the brush; they manipulate it in various ways. The position of the brush tip is carefully controlled to make different strokes. Ink shades play a far more important role than black or grey colours. You will read more about this as you learn the bird-and-flower painting skills step by step following this manual. Again, various strokes and ink applications are best epitomised in bird-and-flower painting.

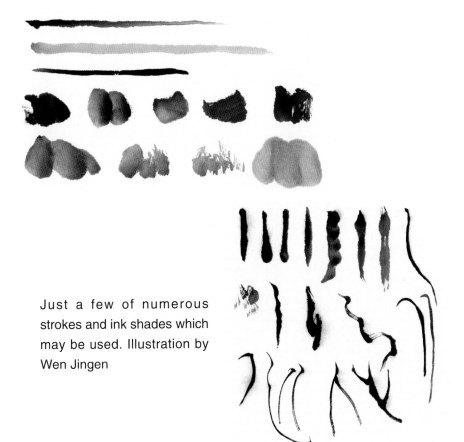

Just a few of numerous strokes and ink shades which may be used. Illustration by Wen Jingen

Exactitude of form is more desirable in figure painting than in bird-and-flower painting. Comparatively speaking, the forms of birds and flowers are simpler than human forms or motifs in landscape. At an early stage of study, students of figure painting must pay close attention to the accuracy of forms and so they cannot have a free hand to exploit the brushwork and ink effects. By practising bird-and-flower painting, they can have a freer approach.

Two Traditions and Different Attitudes towards Artistic Creation

Roughly, Chinese paintings fall into two major categories, the meticulous (*gongbi* 工笔[筆], literally, "meticulous brushwork") and the freestyle (*xieyi* 写[寫]意, literally, "writing ideas"). The former is

Peony, meticulous style, by Wen Jingen

noted for meticulous delineation and strong, brilliant colouring. The latter is noted for bold brushwork, ink application and reduced colour. To be fair, each style has its virtues, and, if executed by incompetent painters, each style may have its weakness. But in the past Chinese scholar-officials, who were virtually amateur artists and also authors of art historical and critical works played up the freestyle and made light of the meticulous style. This prejudice had a strong influence.

Peony, freestyle, by Wen Jingen

Painting manuals (with the *Mustard Seed Garden Manual of Painting* being the most popular), have been published since the 13th century in China. During the centuries, students who learnt from such textbooks in fact concentrated only on one of the two major styles, i.e. freestyle. Many artists who embraced the freestyle tradition at the early stage of their career developed a blind faith in this style and become biased against the other tradition. Once a student of painting embraces this prejudice, he or she tends to pay insufficient attention to technical training.

To guard oneself against this tendency, one should examine the traditional scholar-artists' biased theories in new light.

Many freestyle painters claim that they paint just to "convey their ideas and not aim at formal resemblance". The scholar artist Ni Zan (1301-1374) made a famous statement:

I do bamboo merely to sketch the exceptional exhilaration in my breast, that's all. Then, how can I judge whether it is like something or not, whether its leaves are luxuriant or sparse, its branches slanting or straight? Often when I have daubed and smeared a while, others seeing this take it to be hemp or rushes. Since even I cannot bring myself to argue that it is bamboo, then what of the onlookers? (English translation from Susan Bush, The Chinese Literati on Painting, Harvard University Press, 1971, p. 134)

It is not difficult to refute this fallacy. **That one has some ideas to convey and that one conveys the ideas are not the same thing**. To convey ideas one must resort to some medium and this takes skill. Even the protagonist of literati painting Su Shi (1037-1101) had to admit his incompetence in depiction, a "fault stemming from lack of studying (painting techniques)". If you do not know how to play the piano, you can convey nothing through pressing the keys. If a painting displays meaningless images, can you say it conveys any idea? Please note: only when you put your idea across to the audience, can you say you *convey* it. A person without any training in art can have "exceptional exhilaration" in his breast too. If such a person daubs and smears for a while, can his "painting" *convey* any idea?

Nevertheless, crude and careless representation is not necessarily a trait of the "freestyle" painting that is mainly executed with ink and reduced colour. It is not the manner of expression but the artist's training and attitude towards the creation that determine a painting's quality, as exemplified by two pictures of plum blossom painted in ink respectively by Yan Sou and Gao Qipei, the latter being very famous.

Plum Blossom (detail) by Yan Sou (12th—13th centuries)

This is a truthful portraiture of a plum tree: the petals are tender; the trunk has a rough bark (you can almost feel it!) and the boughs are vigorous.

Plum Blossom by Gao Qipei (1672—1734)

Are you sure the flowers in this picture grow on a plum tree if the artist had not named his painting so? What is the "idea" the artist conveys through those unnamable "flowers"?

With the faults of the corrupted freestyle in mind, readers of this book may steer clear of the bad influence of the amateurish tradition. (Please note: we use the terms of amateurism and professionalism in the sense of standard of perfection. If one works as a full time artist but his or her works show little technical competence, he or she is still an amateur. On the other hand, an artist who supports himself or herself with an occupation other than artistic creation can attain professional standard by constant practice.)

Symbolism

Many bird-and-flower paintings are symbolic. The symbolic interpretation is often derived from homonyms of the subject names. For example, Chinese artists like to paint bamboo because the joint on the bamboo stem is called *jie* in the Chinese language, punning on the word meaning personal integrity. The egret is named *lu si* or *si* for short in Chinese, and *si* may have the meaning of "to think". So a picture of three egrets is the rebus of the saying "think three times", a warning for prudence, derived from the *Analects of Confucius*.

Some symbolic meanings originate in folk beliefs and customs.

Mandarin ducks are believed to be faithful to their spouse and that is why a painting of a pair of this species is a good nuptial present. The magpie is noisy, but Chinese people regard it as a messenger of auspicious news. The bat may be an ugly beast for some peoples, yet part of its name *bianfu* is homonymous with the Chinese word for "fortune", *fu* 福. So it appears in paintings and decorative patterns.

Three Egrets by Lin Fan (b. 1931)

"Three egrets" is a pun of "think three times"

Double Longevity by Yan Bolong (1898-1954)

The Chinese name for the bird paradise flycatcher is *shoudai niao*, the first syllable of which puns on the word *shou* (longevity).

Pine and cranes by Xu Gu (1823-1896)

Pine and cranes are symbols of longevity.

Needless to say, without any knowledge about the symbolic meaning contained in them, bird-and-flower paintings may still be attractive, but with understanding of the embodied meaning, you will be able to place the paintings in context with traditional Chinese culture and hence appreciate them in a new light. Nevertheless, even in ancient times the symbolic meanings for bird-and-flower were secondary and even less so today. Paintings with symbolic meaning make up only a small part of art work produced. If painters pay excessive attention to symbolism in their artistic creation, their work may be reduced to intellectual enigmas.

Do not let symbolism become the main purpose of your creation*. The primary goal of your artistic work is to provide beautiful visual images that appeal directly to the viewers.

Be a Serious Artist

Chinese bird-and-flower is a great tradition but not everything in it is good. One of the bad things is the lack of seriousness of some freestyle painters. They flaunt their casual manner by calling their painting "ink play". Occasionally, a well-trained artist can produce a good work in a playful way. But an artist who treats his creation as a "play" cannot be a good artist. At the end of this foreword we earnestly advice my readers to become conscientious artists. Guo Si, recalls his father, the great 11th-century painter Guo Ruoxu, producing a painting, saying:

To readers who are interested in symbolism in Chinese arts, we recommend C. A. S. Williams, the *Outlines of Chinese Symbolism and Art Motives*, 3rd rev. ed. Dover Publications, 1976, and Fang Jing Pei, *Symbols and Rebuses in Chinese Art: Figures, Bugs, Beasts, and Flowers,* Ten Speed Press, 2004.

I saw my father producing one or two paintings. Sometimes he could not decide how to proceed and then he used to leave them for ten or twenty days. He mulled over them again and again, in no mood to go ahead... When he was inspired and in high spirits, he took them up, forgetting everything around him... When he took up his brush, he would work on a clean table by a bright window, and have incense burning on the right and left of him. He chose good brushes and fine ink sticks. He would wash his hands first, as if he was to meet a distinguished guest... He would often remove what he had painted, add new touches on applied ones, put new strokes on the first ones and then put third strokes on the second ones. Every painting was thus repeatedly elaborated from beginning to end and all over again, as if vigilant against powerful enemies. Only then could he finish his paintings. Does this not show that he never dared to treat his art lightly? I think all things in the world, be it great or small, should be dealt with this way. Only thus can one expect achievement.

Style and Mood

There are many different styles of bird-and-flower painting — from precise to a few simple strokes. The subtle understatement of a simple composition may well appeal to those tuned to Oriental culture, whilst painters in the West often require sharper edges and more detail. In China, paintings often have a feeling of transience, being presented on paper or silk. In the West a more permanent format is often expected. Nowadays there is a greater interest in paper and paper arts, therefore viewers are more comfortable with the fragility of scrolls etc.

Once you have absorbed the techniques in this book, we suggest you find out as much as possible about this genre, along with a style that suits you. Some painters choose exotic birds and flowers, others a more quiet or gentle variety. Colour may appeal to one person, and shape to another painter. Whichever you choose, it should be something you can observe easily and study thoroughly. You need to assess how it grows — a plant does not have to be Chinese and many Western plants originated in China anyway. The same applies to birds — you are probably better off painting a familiar bird to start with as you will be more aware of the movements of that particular bird.

Although it is natural to want to paint a favourite subject, do occasionally try something different. Challenge yourself, and if it does not work, do not immediately say "I cannot do it" as another day you will be in a different mood and it will work well.

Many Chinese paintings incorporate a fine sense of humour. With bird and flower, it is often a look in an eye, or the acrobatics of a particular animal that both appeals and amuses. If something evokes a response, you will have more chance of making it a successful painting. Do not always try the same version but explore the more unusual as well.

A good method of learning is to practice the same subject in all seasons (this also applies for landscape study). Think about how the attitude of the bird may be different, perhaps huddled up against a cold wind or with wings spread out to cool off in the height of summer. Above all you should enjoy your painting study.

Girl and Chickens by Wen Jingen

China's Bird-and-flower Painting: Its Development and Features

China has a long history and the traditional Chinese painting is a gem in Chinese culture.

Bird-and-flower painting is a special genre of Chinese painting. It dates back to patterns on prehistoric pottery and bronze utensils. Judging from their vivid form and the expressiveness of lines, these patterns are rather mature pictures. The bird-and-flower painting as an independent genre emerged later than figure and landscape painting. As it matured, the depiction of various birds and flowers served as a backdrop for human figures — images of birds and flowers were no longer confined to the realm of applied art, but instead, they became objects of aesthetic activities, paving the way for the birth of an independent genre.

Stork and Stone Axe, pattern on prehistoric pottery dating from 5000 years ago, in Henan Provincial Museum

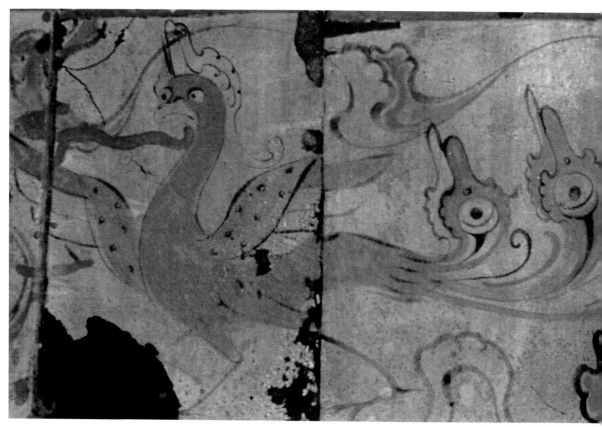

Red Bird, wall painting in tomb, Western Han
Dynasty (206 BC — AD 220)

Birds and Flowers, fragment, colour on paper, unearthed from a Tang-dynasty (AD 618 — 907) tomb in Xinjiang, Northwestern China.

Bird-and-flower painting became independent during the late period of the Tang Dynasty (AD 617—908), the heyday of imperial China. Bian Luan, whose dates are unknown but who was active during the late 8th century, was a master of bird-and-flower painting. He created a new mode of depiction, portraying one or two branches of a flower instead of the whole plant. This ingenious method has been in use until today. During the period of Five Dynasties (AD 908—960), a period of disunion, Xu Xi and Huang Quan created distinct styles of bird-and-flower painting. The former was noted for simplicity and naturalness and the latter for brilliance.

Rare Birds by Huang Quan (d. AD 965)

Bamboo in Snow by Xu Xi

During the Song Dynasty (AD 960—1279), the meticulous style was the mainstream. Birds and flowers were outlined and brilliant colour was placed within the lines. Many masterpieces were created during that time. Zhao Ji (1082—1135) or Emperor Huizong, a poor ruler who lost half of his territory to the Nüzhen (Jurchen) conquerors, was a leading bird-and-flower painter. At the same time, some scholars and Buddhist artists began to promote a shorthand depiction.

Bird on Crab Apple Bough
by Lin Chun (active 1174 — 1189)

Geese and Reeds by Zhao Ji (1082 — 1135)

When the Mongols established the Yuan Dynasty (1279—1368), the free style ink-and-wash painting preferred by the scholar-official painters became the main convention. The motifs of "four gentlemen" (plum, orchid, bamboo and chrysanthemum) dominated bird-and-flower painting and many masters emerged.

Bamboo
by Gao Kegong (1248 — 1310)

Orchid by Zheng Sixiao (124l — 1318)

The ensuing Ming dynasty (1368—1644) saw the emergence of both the freehand style of the royal academy of painting and the freehand style by men of letters. The former was represented by Lin Liang (c. 1416—c. 1480) and the latter, by Xu Wei (1521—1593) and Chen Chun (1483—1544).

Birds (detail) by Lin Liang (c. 1416—c. 1480)

Plum and Bamboo by Sun
Kehong (1532—1611)

Magnolia by Wang Shishen (1686—c.1762)

Bamboo and Chrysanthemum
by Xu Wei (1521—1593)

Bada Shanren (Zhu Da, 1626—1705) further turned the scholars' freehand style into an unrestrained bold expression that exerted great influence on later artists. During the middle part of the Qing Dynasty (1644—1911) the Yangzhou School, or the "Eight Eccentric Artists of Yangzhou", made a breakthrough. Later Zhao Zhiqian (1829—1884), Ren Yi (1840—1896, also known as Ren Bonian) and Wu Changshuo (1844—1927), leaders of the Shanghai School, put forward their graceful and brilliantly coloured paintings to meet the needs of the audience from the international metropolis of Shanghai.

Flowers
by Giuseppe Castiglione
(1688-1766)

Flower by Shi Tao (1641—c.1724)

Lotus Flower
by Bada Shanren (1626-1705)

Giuseppe Castiglione (1688-1766), an Italian Jesuit missionary, spent 51 years in China (mostly in the imperial court) but never had a chance to spread his gospels among the Chinese people. Instead, he contributed many masterpieces of human figures, animals and flowers to Chinese fine arts.

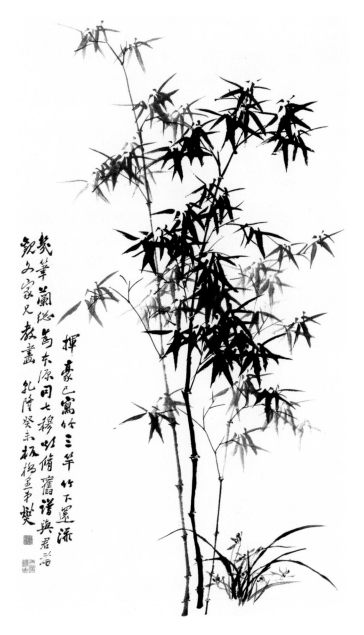

Bamboo by Zheng Xie (1693-1765), one of the "Eight Eccentrics"

Fruit of All Seasons
by Zhao Zhiqian
(1829-1884)

Wild Ducks and Cotton-
rose Hibiscus
by Ren Xun (1835 - 1893)

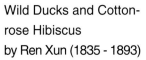

 Peaches
by Wu Changshuo (1844-1927)

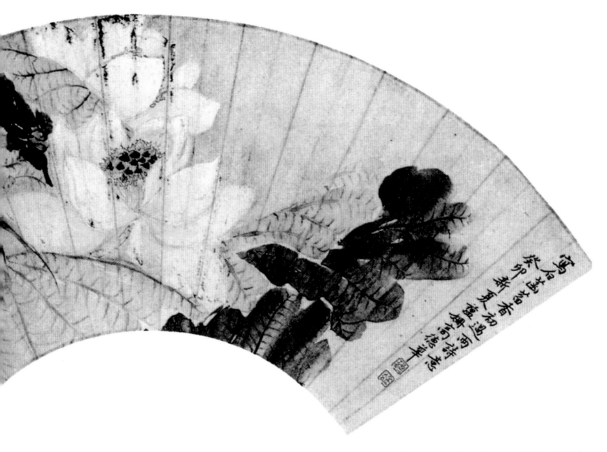

Lotus by Gao Feng (1873-1941)

In the early 20th century, artists in Guangdong borrowed Japanese watercolour techniques for their creation of bird-and-flower painting.

A great master was Qi Baishi (1863—1957) whose works have been praised for the confident and sure handed brushwork plus the overwhelming flavour of everyday life exuding in his images. Later masters include Pan Tianshou (1897—1971), Wang Xuetao (1903—1982), Li Kuchan (1899—1983), Guo Weiqu (1908—1971), Sun Qifeng (b. 1920) and others.

Spring in Southern China
by Chen Shuren (1883-1948)

Hawk
by Gao Jianfu (1879-1951)

Fragrance in Reclusion by Lin Fan (b. 1931)

異香出花枝中有
風霜香寫坡工句
己巳冬 趙炳璃
[印]

Gumbo and Dragonfly
by Zhao Shitong (1847-1945)

Chinese bird-and-flower painting is an embodiment of traditional Chinese aesthetics, ideology and ethics. Traditional Chinese aesthetics may be epitomised by the maxim that the artist "learns from nature meanwhile following his mind". Chinese artists do not try to mimic birds and flowers in nature but make efforts to convey the artists' feelings and emotions through the depicted objects. For example, the "four gentlemen" — the plum, orchid, bamboo and chrysanthemum — have been themes favoured by artists because those plants are believed to assume some special characteristics. Plum blossoms braving snow and freezing wind are unyielding. The bamboo with straight and soaring stems symbolises uprightness and sterling integrity. The orchid exudes fragrance in the wilderness. The chrysanthemum shows her brilliance in biting frost. Also, the peony may symbolise wealth and nobility; the pine, cypress and crane stand for longevity and the lotus that has roots in mud and yet remains clean is a symbol for incorruptible morality. The symbolic meaning of some birds and flowers may be quite different in other cultures. For example, a magpie which is regarded in Chinese art as the bringer of auspicious news, may be a noisy nuisance or an ill omen in other cultures. The symbolic tradition in bird-and-flower painting still lives on today, though symbolism is not the only or foremost motivation of Chinese artists' creation. Nowadays as Chinese society becomes prosperous and Chinese people live a better life, bird-and-flower paintings are created to express the artists' wishes for peace, longevity, constant love and a comfortable life.

Chinese bird-and-flower painting has its special function in cultivation of personalities and aesthetic education, a function not replaceable by other genres. The pleasing atmosphere with beautiful birds and flowers executed in exquisite brushwork and ink may induce a calm and peaceful state of mind to the viewers, and thus

Cats watching Fish
by Cheng Zhang (1869-1938)

refine their mind, inspire their love for life and cultivate their healthy, progressive aspiration. Compared with the figure painting that directly mirrors humankind's struggles against vileness and ignorance, bird-and-flower painting exerts a subtle influence on people's aspiration for beauty, truth and goodness and their hate for ugliness, falsehood and evils.

A salient feature of Chinese bird-and-flower painting is its brushwork and ink. All genres of Chinese painting attach importance to the brushwork and ink application, but bird-and-flower painting, especially in the freehand style, manifests the function of brushwork and ink more compellingly than other genres. The brushwork in freehand bird-and-flower painting is noticeably "calligraphic". Chinese artists often say they "write (brush)" a painting rather than "draw (delineate)" it. This means that they prefer spontaneous, forceful and sure handed strokes to timid retouching. In all the elements of formal beauty, brushwork and ink are the keys. If Chinese ideology is the soul of bird-and-flower painting, brushwork and ink make its body. A soul cannot exist without its body.

Wisteria and Bulbuls
by Ni Tian (1855-1919)

Tools

Photograph by Sun Shuming

Brush

Best brushes are made in Shanlianzhen, Huzhou, Zhejiang Province. With a long history of brush manufacture, this place makes superb brushes with strictly selected materials and sophisticated processing. Some professional painters have brushes made to order there.

When you choose a brush, do not be puzzled by the ornate phrases carved on the brush shafts. Instead, you should consider how the brushes perform. According to the fibres in the brush tip, brushes fall into categories of stiff-fibre, soft-fibre and mixed fibre brushes. Stiff-fibre brushes including weasel-hair (*langhao* 狼毫) and hare-hair (*zihao* 紫毫) are good for drawing lines. Soft-fibre brushes like goat-hair (*yanghao* 羊毫) brushes are good for shading. Mixed-fibre brushes are neither too stiff nor too soft. For a beginner a few stiff-fibre, soft-fibre and mixed-fibre brushes in large, medium and small sizes will do.

Photograph by Sun Shuming

Some new brushes have their fibres glued together. Put the brush in water to remove the glue. After using the brush, wash it clean and hang it on a hanger to dry. When you travel with your brushes, it is best to wrap them in a brush roll (made of split bamboo) and tie the roll tightly, so as to protect the brushes.

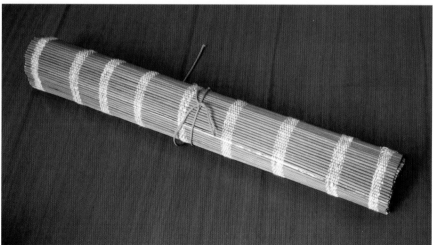

Photographs by Wen Jingen

Telling good brushes from bad brushes

A good brush has following virtues: 1. When wet, a good brush has a pointed tip. 2. When pressed flat, the tip of a good brush is flush. 3. A good brush has a full tip. 4. A good brush has a resilient tip. When you press the brush tip to paper and raise it, the tip resumes its former shape.

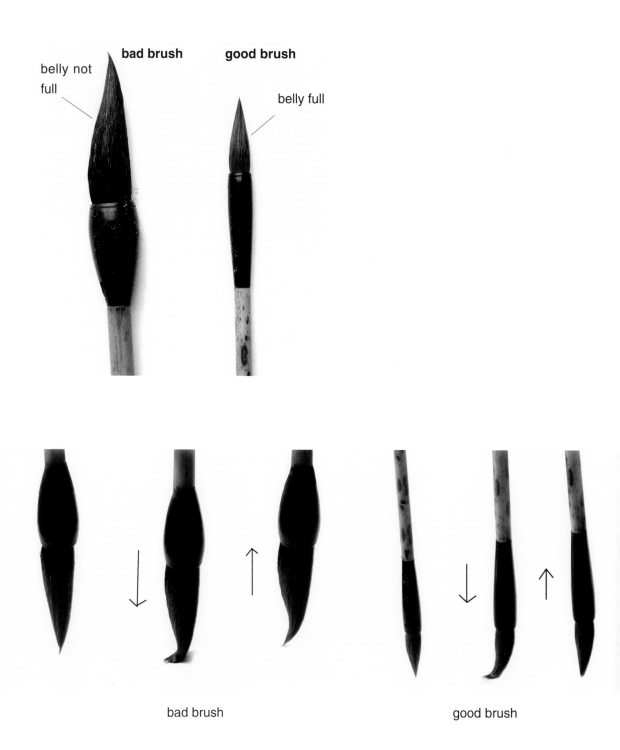

belly not full

bad brush **good brush**

belly full

bad brush

good brush

Illustrations by Wen Jingen

Paper

Use Xuan paper to produce a Chinese painting. Good paper is made in Jingxian County, Anhui Province. Unsized paper is absorbent and gives full rein to ink and colour. Sized paper is processed with alum and is good for meticulous style painting. There are thick and thin unsized papers. Fibres in a good paper are even — including *mianliao danxuan* 棉料单(單)宣, *jingpi* 净(净)皮, *te jingpi* 特净(净)皮, as well as *pizhi* 皮纸(紙) of Wenzhou and *gaolizhi* 高丽(麗)纸(紙). Everyone has a different preference. Once you find a species of paper that suits you, always use this paper — so buy this paper in a larger quantity.

Paintings executed by the author in this book are done on unsized paper.

Ink

In the past Chinese artists used ink sticks. Nowadays, a few artists still grind an ink stick on an ink stone to produce liquid ink, but most artists use bottled ink. Beijing's *Yi De Ge* 一得阁(閣) ink and Shanghai's *Cao Su Gong* 曹素功 ink are good. When using the ink, pour it from the bottle to a dish or ink stone. Ink from the bottle may be too thick, so you may need to add a little water to dilute it. Once the ink in your dish or ink stone becomes dry you should not add water to it and reuse it — wash the dish or ink stone clean and pour in fresh ink.

Photograph by Sun Shuming

Photograph by Wen Jingen

Chinese Bird-and-Flower Painting for Beginners

Colours

Chinese colours fall into categories of "stone colour" and "herbal colour". The former are mineral pigments while the latter vegetable colours. Herbal colours are transparent. Stone colours are mostly body colours, but finely ground stone colours may be transparent as well.

Stone colours are: malachite, azurite, ochre (burnt sienna), vermilion, cinnabar, zinc white, and others.

Herbal colours are: indigo, rattan yellow, rouge, carmine, phthalocynine blue, and others.

Tube colours available in the market are not real Chinese colours. They are chemicals. A beginner may use tube colours, but he or she must keep in his or her mind the difference between them and the traditional Chinese colours. Tube colours are convenient, but they give hues different from genuine Chinese colours.

Colours produced in Jiang Sixu Tang 姜思序堂 are of best quality.

Colours can be mixed. When mixing colours, do not stir them thoroughly. Different shades in your strokes may be more appealing than thoroughly mixed, even and flat ones.

Photograph by Sun Shuming

Genuine Chinese colour

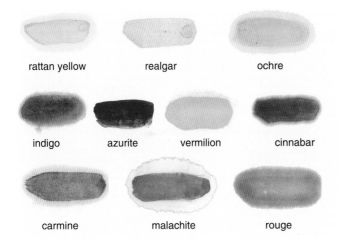

rattan yellow	realgar	ochre

indigo	azurite	vermilion	cinnabar

carmine	malachite	rouge

Tube colour

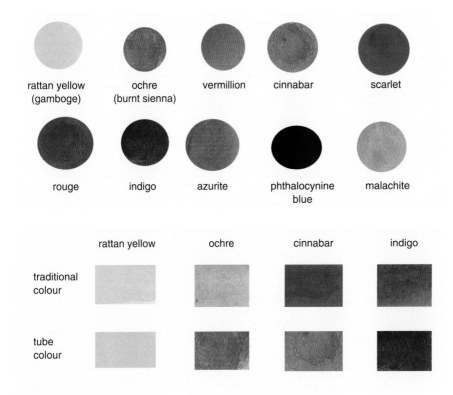

rattan yellow (gamboge)	ochre (burnt sienna)	vermillion	cinnabar	scarlet

rouge	indigo	azurite	phthalocynine blue	malachite

	rattan yellow	ochre	cinnabar	indigo
traditional colour				
tube colour				

Illustrations by Wen Jingen

Accessories

Painting felt is to support the paper on the table. Without a piece of felt under the unsized paper, ink and colour will run through the paper onto the table, come back into the paper and make a blot.

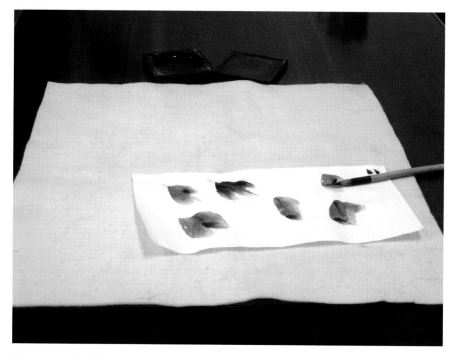

Illustration by Wen Jingen

It is better to have two **bowls for washing brushes**. One bowl for washing warm colours (red, yellow, ochre, etc.) and the other for washing cool colours (blue, green, ink, etc.)

A **palette** is convenient when you work outside, but when working at home, Chinese artists like using separate white dishes to contain and mix colours. You should have a large dish for mixing ink. A bowl of clean water is necessary. When you need pure colours, you must use clean water but not the water in the bowl for washing brushes.

Photograph by Sun Shuming

Paperweights are used to keep the paper flat and in position — this will prevent the brush missing the paper.

Seals, photograph by Sun Shuming

Seal impressions, photograph by Sun Shuming

Brushwork, Ink and Colour Skills

Centre-tip stroke. Hold the brush vertically and keep the brush tip at the centre of the stroke.

Illustration by Wen Jingen

Side-tip stroke. Hold the brush at a slant and keep the brush tip at one side of the stroke.

Illustration by Wen Jingen

A centre-tip stroke looks full, vigorous and robust. A side-tip looks vivid and pliable. But they have both their disadvantages too. If not well controlled, a centre-tip stroke may become rigid and a side-tip stroke may be insipid. Experienced artists use both types of strokes.

The brush tip can be concealed within the stroke or exposed. In bird-and-flower painting, strokes with the trace of the brush tip exposed are often used.

Reverse the brush tip. At the end of a stroke, slightly turn the brush tip backward, i.e. at the end of a stroke moving to the left, turn the brush tip slightly to the right and at the end of a downward stroke, turn the brush tip slightly upward, and vice versa.

Start a stroke by moving the brush tip to the left a little

Turn the brush tip to the right and move it

Illustration by Wen Jingen

Begin a stroke by moving the brush tip to the left

Centre-tip, side-tip and reverse-tip strokes (the dark line shows the movement of the brush tip point)

Move the brush to the right

At the end of the stroke, turn the brush tip towards the left again

Result: a stroke with the trace of the brush tip concealed at the both ends
Illustrations by Wen Jingen

Upward

Turn

Downward

Result: a round dot

Illustrations by Wen Jingen

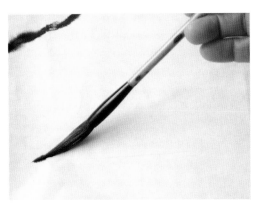

Drag the brush. Let the brush tip lie on paper and pull the brush away from the mark. This kind of brushwork can be used to depict messy grass and brambles.

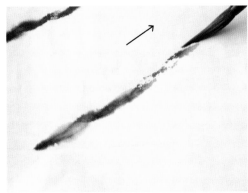

Illustration by Wen Jingen

Contour. In meticulous painting, the centre-tip stroke is used to contour objects. In freehand painting, centre-tip and side-tip strokes are both used. Some strokes may have hiatus but the whole stroke still looks complete. Gentle and forceful strokes should be employed alternately. Strokes should be confident and neat.

Contoured orchid leaves. From *Mustard Seed Garden Manual of Painting*

A broken stroke may appear continuous. 意到笔(筆)不到

When a painter is well versed in brushwork he may work rapidly. In rapid and confident movement of the brush, sometimes the brush tip may skim over the paper surface leaving an unpainted place. Yet the stroke appears complete and continuous. This effect appears in English calligraphy too. Note that this effect is achieved inadvertently. Do not produce such strokes deliberately. (Gombrich in his *Art and Illusion*, p. 209, misinterpreted this saying [inaccurately rendered in English as "when idea present, brush may be spared of performance"] as purposeful omission of details in depiction.)

From *Mustard Seed Garden Manual of Painting.* Note two blades have a hiatus yet they appear continuous.

Dot. Usually the brush is held perpendicular to the paper. Raise your arm above the table. If your elbow rests on the table, you cannot move your hand freely. This is very important for producing free and expressive dots.

Illustrations by Wen Jingen

Dot strokes are the most frequently used device in bird-and-flower painting. Often the brush is loaded with different shades of ink or colours. Petals and leaves of flowers, the heads and backs of birds are often depicted with dotting. Do not retouch your dots.

Illustration by Wen Jingen

There are two ways of applying colours. The first way is to cover the whole inked picture with a thin layer of colour wash. The colour layer is transparent and does not cover the ink strokes under it. The other way is to fill colours into inked contours.

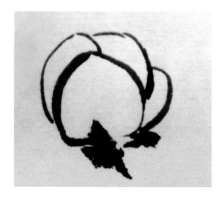

Ink contoured painting

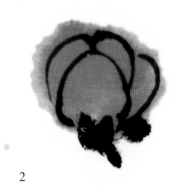

1. Cover with a layer of colour
2. Result
3. Ink contoured painting
4. Fill the contour with colour
5. Result

Illustrations by Wen Jingen

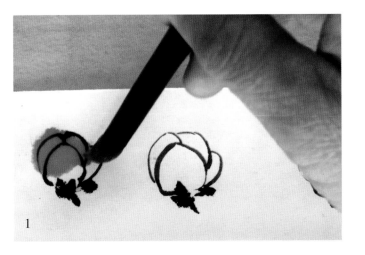

Texture-stroke (*cun* 皴) is a light, dry stroke that sets off a rough surface like that of a tree trunk or stone. It is used mainly in landscape painting. In bird-and-flower painting it can be used to depict birds' feathers or rocks.

texture strokes

Illustration by Wen Jingen

A **skimming stroke** (*ca* 擦) is akin to the texture-stroke except it is even drier. It is rarely used in bird-and-flower painting.

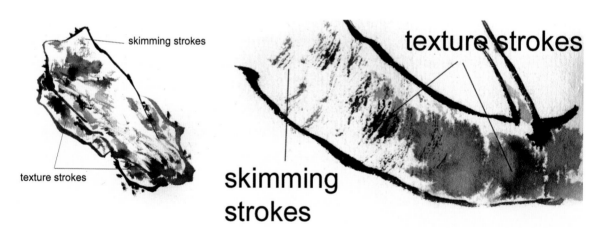

skimming strokes

texture strokes

texture strokes

skimming strokes

Illustrations by Wen Jingen

Rock and Chrysan-
themum (detail)
by Zou Yigui (1686-1772)

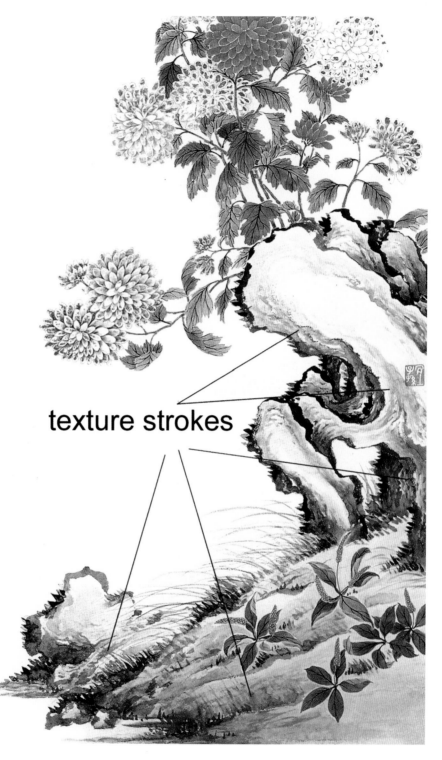

texture strokes

Wet on wet. When the first stroke is still wet, put on another mark, letting the second stroke spread on the first one. You can put dark ink on light ink and you can also put light on dark ink. This method applies for colour too.

dark on light   light on dark

second touch too early   **second touch too late**

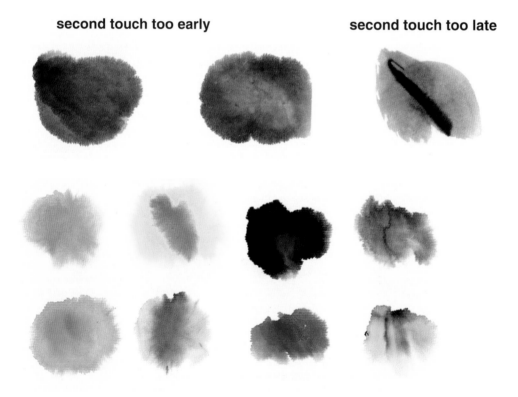

Illustrations by Wen Jingen

Splash ink. Use a broad-tipped brush and saturate it with ink and make unrestrained strokes.

Loofah, depicted in splash ink by Wen Jingen

Accumulated ink strokes (a stock device in landscape painting) are occasionally used in bird-and-flower painting.

Illustration by Wen Jingen

You can load your brush with light ink or colour. Before you put it onto paper, dip the brush point in dark ink or another colour and immediately put the brush onto paper. In this way you will acquire a stroke that has different shades of ink or colours.

Load the brush with light ink

Dip the brush point in dark ink

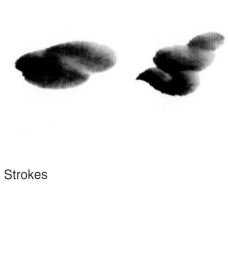

Strokes

Illustrations by Wen Jingen

Dip the brush point in colour after loading it with ink

Strokes

Illustrations by Wen Jingen

Ink has five colours. 墨分五色

Contrast of dark and light, as well as wet and dry, strokes produce a unity in variance. Dry and wet strokes must be combined. Water is the key for gradations of ink and colours.

Illustration by Wen Jingen

Approaches to Bird-and-flower Painting: Copying, Painting From Life, From Memory, and Studying Masterpieces

Copying masterpieces has been a major traditional method of teaching Chinese painting. Chinese painting has its own rich vocabulary that can be learned through copying. It is better to copy from the original work. If original paintings are not available, good quality prints may be used. Do not use poorly printed pictures or small prints. Your copy should be the size of the original. Do not copy hastily. Before you set your brush on paper, carefully study the stroke sequence of the original painting — its brushwork and ink application. Only with a good understanding of the original's execution and brushwork and ink can you make a successful copy.

Beginners often copy from the originals. As you make progress in copying, I recommend copying masterpieces from your memory. This will compel you to analyse and study the original work in more depth, with more care and eventually lead you to independent creation. Copying from the original and copying from the memory can be done alternately.

Life is the teacher of all artists. Without life, art will become water without a source or a tree without a root. Traditional Chinese painting teaching attached too much importance to copying and paid insufficient attention to painting from life. In fact only through painting from life can an artist understand the relationship between the forms in nature and forms in art, and have his or her initiative in artistic creation.

Artistic images are results of processing in the artist's head. In art some parts in nature are enhanced or emphasised and other parts are subdued or omitted. In face of the colours of nature, a beginner must have a selective eye. He or she should not copy everything in sight, but instead should discover the beauty hidden in nature and choose suitable parts. In painting flowers, he or she need not paint the whole plant. A few branches may do. His or her work should basically imitate nature but not slavishly copy it.

Beginners can sketch with pen or pencil in a sketchbook. In doing so, a beginner should pay attention to the use of lines. Hatching is seldom used.

一九八七年九月十日玉渊潭写生

Rose, sketch in ink
by Wen Jingen

Iris, sketch in pencil
by Wen Jingen

Painting from memory is very important. However fast you work, you cannot capture the image of a bird in flight. But you can paint it from memory. Painting from memory is a fine tradition in Chinese arts. One cannot work from memory before one has spent time in painting from life. You must not fabricate images on a whim. Painting from memory is a way leading to independent artistic creation.

Studying paintings is not the same thing as viewing paintings. In studying a painting, you should try to answer many questions. Is the picture in a vivid atmosphere? Is it suggestive? Are the brushwork and ink application good? Is the colouring fine? Is its composition expressive? Are the inscription and seal impressions appropriately added? Through studying paintings you will hone your judgment and improve your artistic quality. An artist with good understanding of masterpieces makes quick progress. Do not miss any opportunity to study good paintings. It is best to take notes while viewing good works. At the beginning, your teacher's advice may help you resist bad art.

Painting Flowers

Before you paint flowers, you must study their forms and characteristics. Observe the structure of their branches, leaves and flowers plus their relationship between each other.

With all this in mind, you will be able to paint a likeness of them. When you produce a painting, you should have the whole picture in your mind. Let your mind direct your hand.

Traditional teaching of bird-and-flower painting starts with the "four gentlemen" — the plum blossom, bamboo, orchid and chrysanthemum.

Mustard Seed Garden Manual of Painting

芥子园(園)画(畫)传(傳)

This manual, completed and printed 1679-1701, has been a very popular textbook for beginners. It not only explains the skills for painting flowers, figures and landscape, giving step-by-step illustrations, but also contains the main points on painting criticism as well. In ancient China when art historical and critical works were beyond the reach of common people, the manual played an important role in disseminating knowledge about painting and art criticism. Needless to say, the manual has some biased views. For example, it holds that meticulously delineated painting cannot possess a vivid atmosphere. An English translation by Mai-mai Sze, under the title *The Tao of Painting*, with the translator's own study in theoretical issues, is still available in many libraries. Unfortunately this translation is based on an early 20th-century lithography edition and the monochrome edition has lost the ink shades and colours of the original block-printing edition.

Snow on Bamboo, from the
*Mustard Seed Garden
Manual of Painting* — the
block printing edition.

Snow on Bamboo, from the
*Mustard Seed Garden
Manual of Painting*,
lithography edition. The
snow is gone!

Orchid

There is a formula concerning the arrangement of orchid leaves: long, short and crossing. The first stroke is long, the second, short and the third crosses the first stroke. These three strokes make a basic unit.

Repeat this unit and you will have rhythmically arranged leaves.

Orchid petals can be contoured or depicted with broad strokes. As the leaves are painted in dark ink, the petals should be in light ink so as to produce a contrast. The petals should be in gradated ink.

Depicting orchids in ink is a good basic exercise. Practise repeatedly until you can subconsciously paint each leaf and petal. Your brushwork should be flowing, natural and relaxed. Affected performance of the brush and ink is undesirable.

Distinguish different species of orchids. One species has only one flower on a stem, whilst another species, *Cymbidium faberi*, has several alternate flowers on each stem.

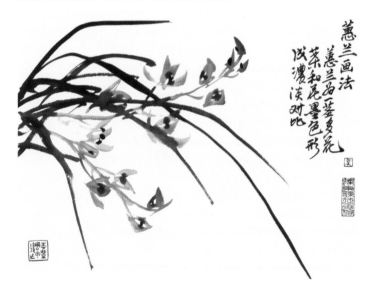

Once you learn to depict orchids with ink, you can substitute the ink with ochre or rouge. You can also paint orchids with outline or solid strokes.

Red orchid by Joseph Shan Pao Lo (1922-1998 late president of the Chinese Brush Painters Society in the UK)

Plum blossom

Steps: painting a plum flower

Illustrations by Wen Jingen

Paint the main trunks and branches. Let boughs cross each other so that some of them appear in the front while others are at the back. In arranging the branches, avoid parallel lines. Three lines crossing each other at one point also looks awkward.

Draft in charcoal

When depicting the trunk of an old tree, use more dry strokes than wet. Paint some tender branches long while others are short. Employ leftward, rightward, upward and downward strokes. Use both centre-tip and side-tip strokes. Do not use too strong or too pale ink to depict the trunks.

Depict the petals with dots of white mixed with carmine or rouge. Try to conceal the brush tip in the dots so that they appear round. In some places the petals are denser than in others. Do not arrange flowers evenly through the plane of the picture. The colour of the petals should be in different shades.

Use a small weasel-hair brush to depict the stamens and calyx with dark ink or dark ink mixed with rouge. The small dots show flowers at different angles.

Steps
by Wen Jingen

Petals of plum blossom can be depicted with coloured dots. White flowers are often outlined. Over the ink contour, green lines may be added so as to make the petals look thick and full. After that, fill colour into the contours. When contouring a petal, the brushwork should be free and spontaneous.

In the past, men of letters liked to depict plum blossoms in ink. The trunk is painted in dark ink, the petals in light ink, and the dots on trunks in very dark ink.

Plum Blossom in Ink by Wan Shanglin, 1814

You may also add colour to a painting shown purely in ink. Do not apply the colour evenly. Present the petals in different shades.

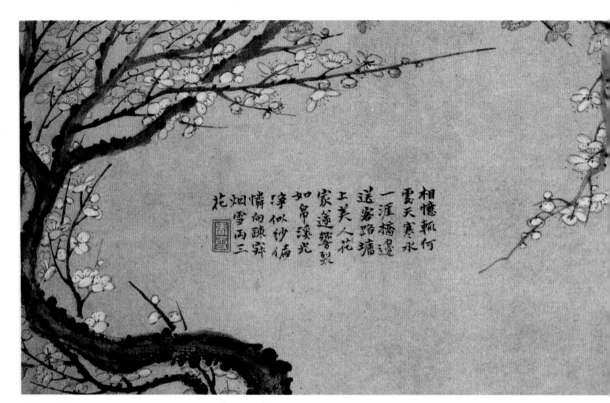

Plum Blossom by Luo Fangshu, 18th or 19th century

Bamboo

Who created the ink bamboo painting?

An anecdote attributes the method of painting bamboo with ink to a Lady Li who lived during the Five Dynasties (AD 907-960). It is said that one night she saw the shadow cast by bamboo in moonlight on a window and traced the shadow with an ink brush. In fact historical documents have records of ink bamboo created during the Tang Dynasty (AD 618-907). So Lady Li's "invention" — if she did find the technique by herself at all, — was a repeated invention. Extant works point to Wen Tong (1018-1079) as a master of ink bamboo. Painters of ink bamboo emerged in great numbers during the Yuan Dynasty (1279-1368).

Ink Bamboo by Wen Tong

When depicting a bamboo stem, reinforce both the beginning and ending of a stroke by stopping the brush and pressing it with more force so as to make the ends of a stroke thicker, in the shape of a joint. In the middle part of a stroke, force must be applied evenly. Avoid parallel stems.

Start a section of bamboo stem by pressing the brush tip slightly

Move the brush

At the end of the section of stem, press the brush tip slightly again

Lift the brush from paper

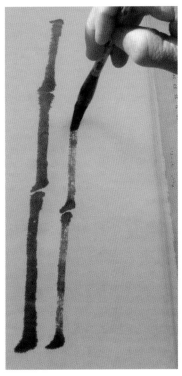

Start another section

Step illustrations by Wen Jingen

Bamboo branches must be coherent but they need not be joined with each other. You can depict leaves after the branches or the vice versa. Move your brush quickly.

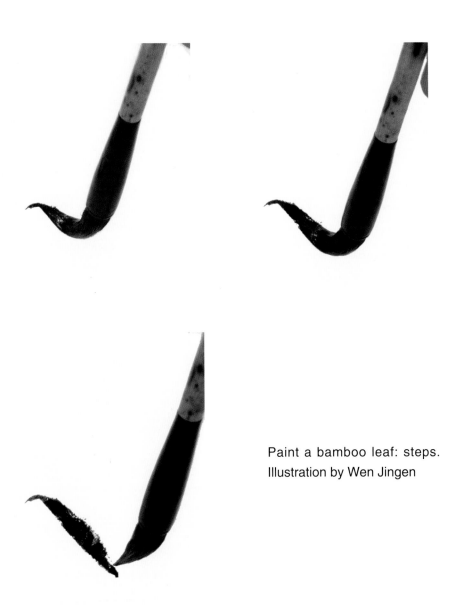

Paint a bamboo leaf: steps.
Illustration by Wen Jingen

Leaves may be grouped as shown in this picture. Bamboo leaves in the background may be painted in light ink and those in the foreground, in dark ink. Depict the leaves at the edge of a grove more distinctly than the leaves within the grove.

 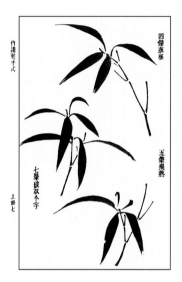

Forms of bamboo leaves (from *Mustard Seed Garden Manual of Painting*)

Try a few leaves. Illustration by Wen Jingen

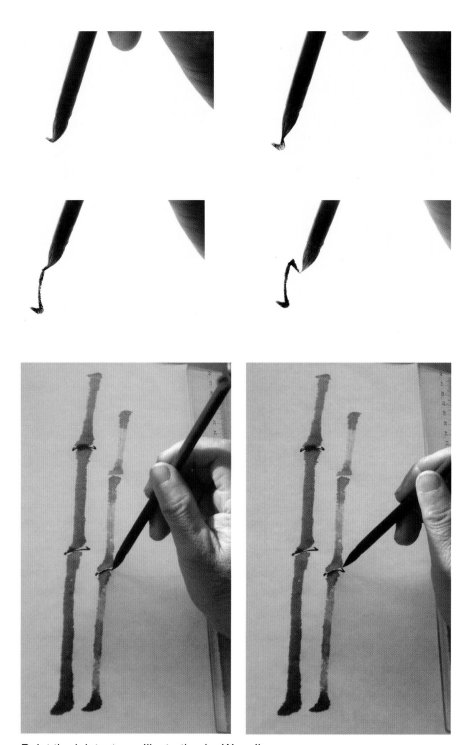

Paint the joint: steps. Illustration by Wen Jingen

Draft the whole picture with charcoal or a pencil. — This step is necessary for beginners. You can wipe off the charcoal marks when ink is applied. If you draft with a pencil, use a light pencil.

Depicting bamboo is a proper basic training for bird-and-flower painters. The brushwork used in painting bamboo has many common features with depiction of other plants.

Step illustrations by Wen Jingen

Painting a strong bamboo stem

You can use a flat tip brush to paint a strong bamboo stem. Load the brush with light ink and then load the two sides of the brush tip with dark ink.

Load the brush with light ink   Load the two sides of the brush tip with dark ink

Result. Illustrations by Wen Jingen

Chrysanthemum

Chrysanthemum flowers are usually outlined. The petals should be long or short and in several layers. Do not paint a flower in a wheel-shaped circle. Make frontal views, side views and back views of the flowers. Depict buds and half blooming flowers.

The chrysanthemum is a herbaceous plant and its branches are tender, so do not use dry strokes to depict the branches. The leaves should be shown with ink in different shades.

When two flowers are depicted side by side, paint one flower in full view and the other in partial view; paint the first in detail and the second sketchily. When painting the leaves press the brush onto the paper, sometimes to its heel.

When the ink strokes are dry, add colour. Most chrysanthemum flowers are yellow. You can also use carmine, rouge and vermilion. Do not add the colour into the petals too neatly — let it flow beyond the lines occasionally. White chrysanthemum flowers may have light green lines added to the ink marks. You may also add white colour to the contoured flower.

Peach blossom

Depict branches first. Leave spaces for the flowers.

Step 1: depict the branches. But before you add ink strokes, I recommend that you draft the whole picture with charcoal or a pencil.

Add petals with dot strokes. Mix white with carmine. Note that plum petals are round and peach blossom petals are pointed.

Add green leaves. Some tender leaves may be painted with green mixed with a little rouge.

Step 2

When the petals are dry, add stamens and calyxes with ink and white. When leaves are half dry, add veins with dark ink.

Step 3
Illustrations by Wen Jingen

Paint a peach flower: steps:

Paint petals with dots. Note the position of the brush tip points to the outside of the flower

Add stamens with ink (or ink mixed with rouge) strokes

Add white (or pale yellow) for the pollen dots

Result

Step illustrations by Wen Jingen

Peach blossoms with multiple corollas are very beautiful.

Photographs by Wen Jingen

Here are the steps for painting a multiple corolla peach flower:

Add outer petals with darker colour.　　More outer petals

Add the stamens with white or pale yellow   Add pistils

Step illustrations by Wen Jingen

Steps for painting a multiple corolla peach blossom branch:

Step 1: draft with charcoal or a pencil.
Beginners do not skip over this step

Step 2: paint with ink strokes and add
texture strokes on the trunk and boughs.

Step 3: add flowers and leaves

Step 4: add pistils and stamens. Illustrations by Wen Jingen

Iris

Paint the petals of iris with blue or purple colour. You can use phthalocynine blue or azurite. Purple may be attained by mixing phthalocynine blue and rouge. Load the brush tip with white and then dip it in blue or purple. The brush tip loaded this way makes gradated strokes.

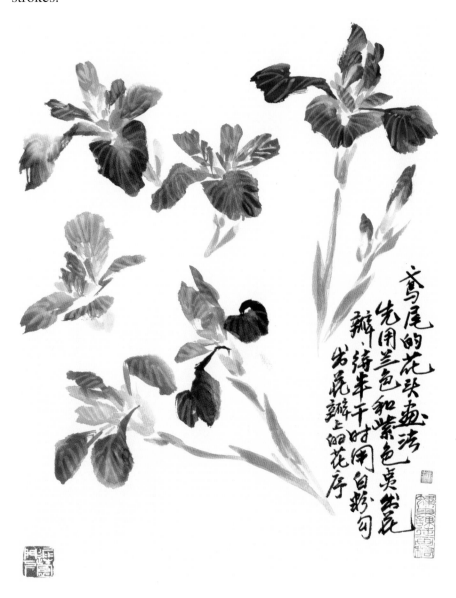

Paint the leaves with herbal green (a mixture of indigo and rattan yellow). Before the leaves are dry, outline them with ink lines. The ink contours do not need to be complete for each leaf blade.

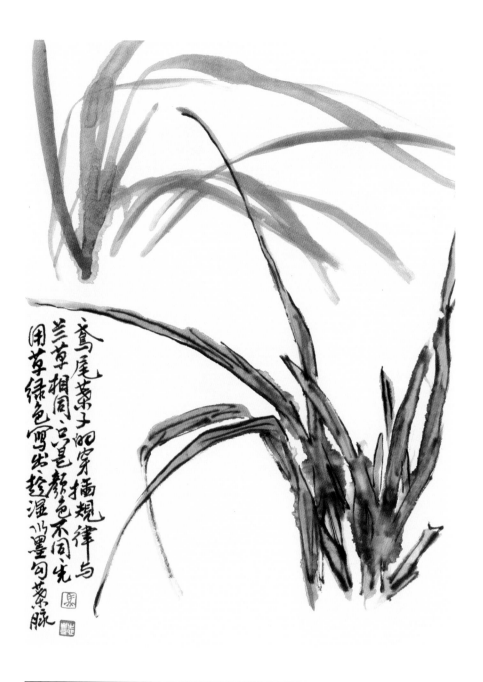

Paint the leaves and flowers with colour. Please note that the colour of the stalks is different from that of the leaves. The colour used to depict the stalks is a mixture of herbal green (indigo and rattan yellow) and ochre.

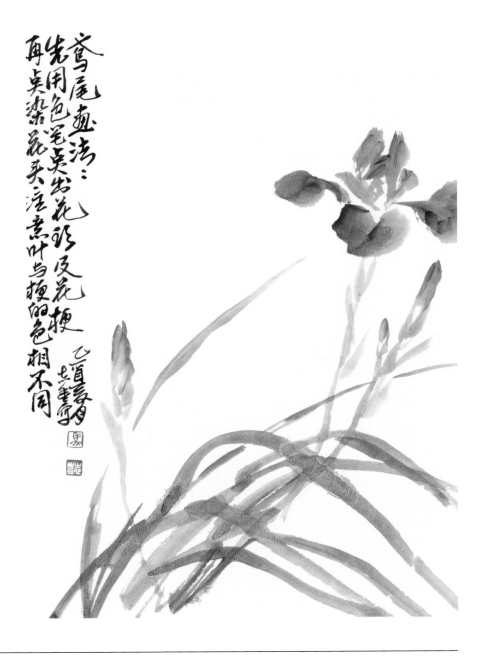

While the strokes are still wet, delineate the major veins on the petals with white. The white strokes need not be distinct. Paint the stamens at the centre of the flowers with yellow colour. Because the flower and leaves are all in cool colour, it is better to add some warm colour on the background.

Day lily

Chinese painters like painting the day lily because it is the name-sake of another grass that is believed to be able to relieve one's sorrows. The day lily is also a symbolism of older ladies.

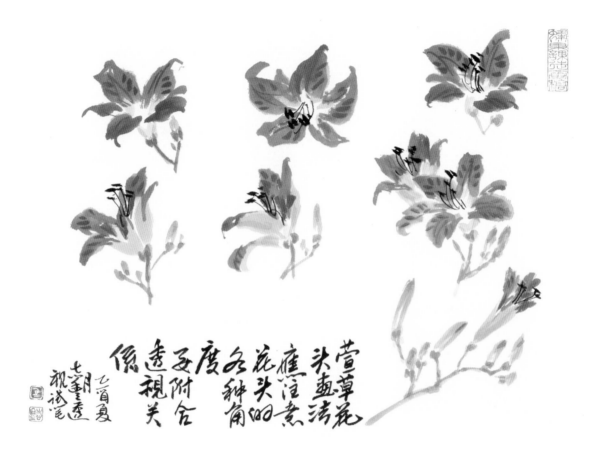

When you depict a day lily flower, show the difference between the front and back sides of a petal by using different colours. This is more important in the depiction of half-blooming flowers. Paint the back side of a petal with rattan yellow mixed with vermilion. The front side of a petal is tinted with vermilion and carmine.

The leaves are herbal green that contains more indigo than yellow.
While the leaves are still wet, add the main veins with dark ink.

Banana

Render the central veins of leaves first. Add broad strokes to depict the leaves. The strokes should not be parallel. They should be in different lengths and shades.

When the leaves are half dry or still wet, add veins in dark ink. Again parallel lines should be avoided.

Lotus

When depicting lotus leaves, try to display their turns and folds. In large areas of ink, the brushwork should be vigorous. Limp strokes are undesirable. Some dry strokes added to large wet strokes appear spirited.

There are several ways to depict the flower. White flowers are outlined and coloured. Light green strokes can be added to the ink lines. Red flowers can be painted with rouge or carmine. The colour at the root of a petal is lighter than that at the tip of a petal.

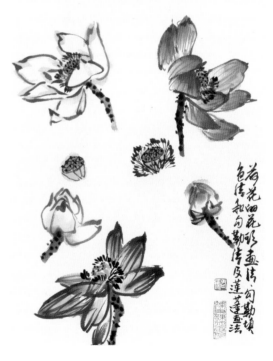

You can use ink to depict lotus leaves, and you can also add indigo or herbal green (mixture of indigo and rattan yellow) onto the dry ink strokes. Try to show the distance between the leaves in the foreground and those in the background. When the whole painting is dry, add some grass leaves with dark ink. Lines and broad patches of colour produce an interesting contrast.

Another method to depict lotus leaves — render the outline and veins with dark ink and before the strokes become dry, apply herbal green to the ink so that the ink shades into the green. White flowers can be set off with large leaves.

Wisteria

Wisteria branches cross each other like plum branches. The difference is that wisteria branches are in curved lines instead of straight lines.

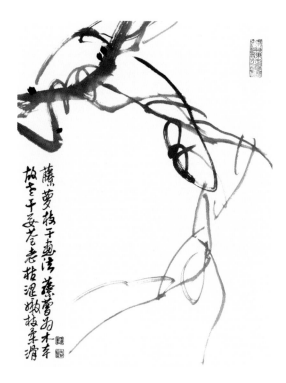

When the branches are done, add flowers with purple colour. Use wet strokes to set off the tactile value of the flower petals.

Add leaves. The leaves are in warm green colour — add some ochre to herbal green. Before you put the brush onto the paper, pick up a little rouge on the tip.

The purple used to depict the flower is gained by mixing indigo or phthalocynine blue or azurite with rouge and white. The purple may have a red or blue tinge.

Laburnum by Pauline Cherrett

Chinese Trumpet Creeper

The flower can be depicted in cinnabar or vermilion mixed with carmine. The brushwork should be confident. The leaves may be painted with ink or herbal green. Depict the leaf veins with dark ink and the stamens with dried-up ink.

The branches are like those of wisteria. Usually these are executed before any flowers are added.

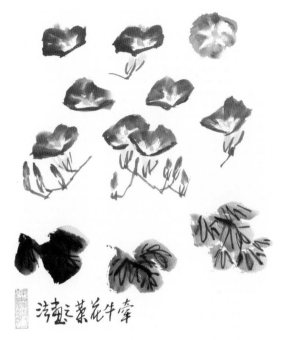

Morning glory

The flower of the morning glory may be pink, blue or purple. Depict the flower with colour strokes. The centre of the flower is left blank so that it appears an empty space. Each leaf has three points and can therefore be depicted using three strokes.

The morning glory is an herbaceous plant, so its vines are unlike those of the woody plants such as wisteria. You may depict its flowers first and then join them with vines.

Calabash

The calabash can be shown contoured or by using solid strokes. Use yellow or green colour. Try to accentuate its volume.

Beans

The bean is a vegetable vine plant. The strokes need not be joined to each other but they should be coherent. Move your brush quickly.

Peony

The peony has two subspecies: tree and herbaceous. The tree species is called *mudan* 牡丹 in Chinese and the herbaceous, *shaoyao* 芍药. They look alike except that the herbaceous plant's leaves are narrower and longer than those of the tree subspecies.

Paint a flower in four steps as shown in the illustration. Paint the central part of a flower with white mixed with carmine. Wash the brush clean or use another brush, load it with carmine and paint the surrounding petals. The deep places at the root of the petals can be painted with dark rouge.

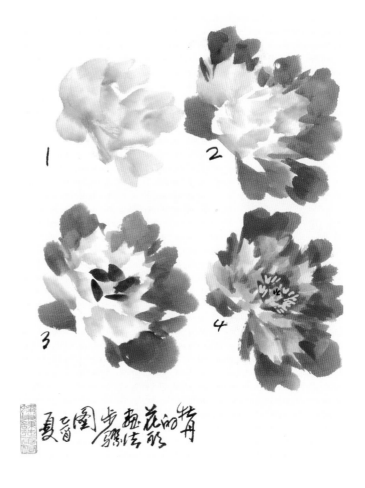

Do not make the outline of a flower round. Extending petals should have angular contours. The whole flower should be in dark, light and transitional shades.

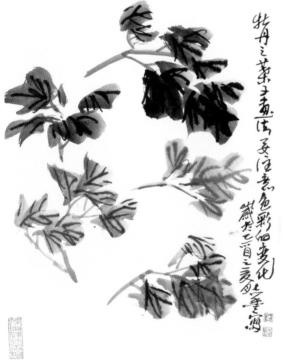

A leaf of the peony has three prongs. In proper perspective they appear in different shapes and sizes. The colour of the leaves is mainly herbal green (rattan yellow mixed with indigo). But the green can be in different shades. Lush leaves can be painted with green mixed with ink; tender leaves can have a tinge of rouge and withered leaves may contain ochre.

The boughs of the peony can be painted with ink, and the tender branches, in green tinted with rouge. Depict old boughs with dry strokes and tender branches, with wet strokes. Buds are at the end of new branches.

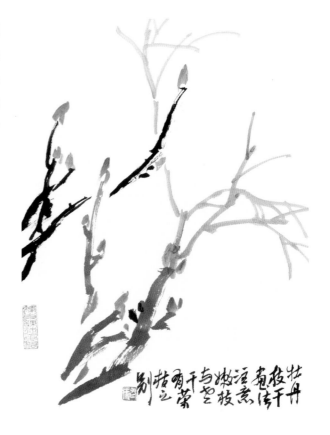

The broad leaves and petals contrast with the narrow strokes of the branches making a symphony of surfaces and lines. A painting with two groups of dark leaves appears as a balanced composition.

Some artists paint the peony all in ink. Light ink is used to depict flower petals and dark ink is used to depict leaves.

The herbaceous peony has similar flowers to the tree peony, but the leaves of the former are narrower and longer than those of the latter.

Contour the white flower of the peony with centre-tip brushstrokes. After contouring in ink, ochre lines can be added on the ink lines. White colour may be applied to the petals on the back side of the paper.

Rose

Rose flowers can be painted with dots. Its opposing leaves are saw-toothed. Its branches are thorny.

White roses can be contoured with lines. Yellow roses can be out-lined and coloured. The yellow may have a tinge of vermilion.

Painting Birds

Chinese artists have a saying, "The shape of a bird is not far away from an egg". The overall outline of a bird is oval. Folk painters also compared the proportion of a bird's head and body to a date and an egg.

Different positions of the head and neck determine the posture of a bird. The views of birds are in four categories: back view with the head on top, back view with the head at bottom, frontal view with the head on top and frontal view with the head at bottom.

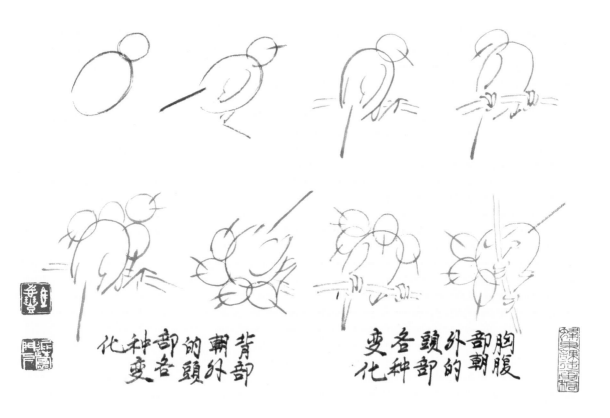

Myna bird

Paint a myna bird in six steps as shown in the picture. In the last step, use light ink to bring different parts of the bird into a whole.

Depict the breast and belly of a myna with two strokes. The upper part of the stroke is darker than the bottom. Multiple trivial strokes are undesirable.

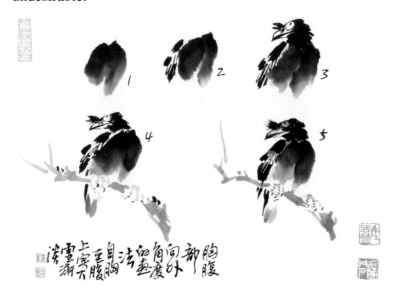

Show the myna bird's head in a proper perspective. To depict the beak, you must stop the brush tip momentarily to reinforce the beginning of the first stroke.

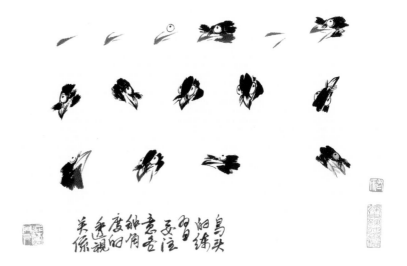

Paint the bird's legs and claws with "calligraphic" strokes. Leave small blanks at the joints of the legs. Pay attention to the different poses of the legs and claws.

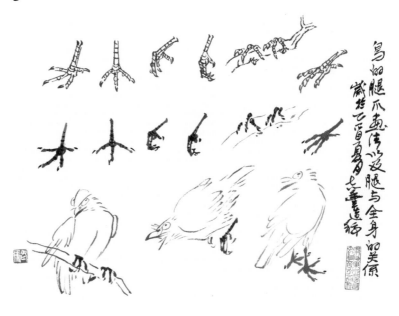

When you depict two birds perching on a bough, put them in different poses. If one of them is in a frontal view, the other may be in a back view. If one stands upright, the other may sit horizontally. If one is in motion, the other may be still. If one is fully portrayed, the other may be partly hidden behind some objects, and so on.

When you grasp the skill to depict the myna in easier poses, you may try to paint the bird in complicated actions, like preening feathers, frolicking, fighting, and preying on insects.

Once you have learned to paint birds in a stationary pose, try to paint them in motion. Observe birds in nature, study and copy good works so as to have a command of the movements of a bird.

Process the bird's form artistically. Angular contours look more spirited than round ones.

Magpie

The illustration shows the similarity between the myna and the magpie.

In Chinese language, "magpies perching on a plum tree" is homonymous with the phrase "joy shown at the eyebrows".

Oriole

The oriole is a medium-sized bird, like the myna. Contour the oriole and depict the spots on its wings with ink dots. When the ink strokes are dry, add some yellow. Note that the colour on its shoulders and back is stronger (add some ochre in the rattan yellow) than on its belly. Its legs and claws can be painted with carmine.

Turtledove

Paint the head and back with a mixture of ink and ochre. Before the first strokes are dry, add ink dots. When the ink is dry, add a layer of shade three (Label three) of azurite. The layer of azurite should not be too thick; otherwise it will cover the other colours. The beak, legs and claws can be painted with carmine or vermilion. Apply thick white dots at the neck. Do not let the white dots cover the ink dots.

Quail

Paint the quail with ink strokes and add ink dots on the head and back. Depict the belly and when the line is dry, add ochre. Paint some indigo marks onto its shoulders and light rattan yellow on its belly.

Mandarin duck

In Chinese culture, the mandarin duck is a symbol of constant love between man and wife. They often appear in pairs in paintings.

First, paint the crest, beak and eyes with dark ink. Render the feathers on its cheeks with light ink strokes. Add strong ink dots on its back. Paint the wings with ink lines. Depict the feathers at the root of the tail with dry and light strokes. Paint the breast and the end of the tail with dark ink. When the ink is dry, paint the beak and feet with vermilion or orange, shade the pupil with light purple, and paint the feathers with vermilion or carmine (at the neck), yellow (the feathers on the wing) and indigo (on the back). When the indigo is dry, add some malachite dots. The ink marks are the key to a successful representation of the mandarin duck. The female mandarin duck is painted with light ink and coloured with ochre. The dull plumage gives a contrast with the brilliance of the male bird's feathers.

Hawk

The hawk is bird of prey. When you paint a hawk, try to present its character. Accentuate the hooked beak and claws — they are weapons in capturing game. It is best to render the eye squarish rather than round. The upper eyelid is a straight line, not a curve, because it is thick and the eye socket is deep. Paint the shoulder with light ink and when the ink is still wet, add dots in dark ink. Paint the plume and tail with dark ink.

The hawk can turn its head without moving its body. Paint the head when the body is done.

Crane

Paint the crane's body first, and then its head and neck. Add light ochre mixed with ink and finally paint the eye and beak. Show the legs with centre-tip strokes in dark ink. Note that its tail is hidden under the long black plumes.

This crane stands with its belly facing the viewer. The legs and claws are executed with calligraphic strokes. The black plumes should be rendered with spirited strokes.

Peacock

A good under-painting in ink is of crucial importance — use lines and dots. The neck is painted with dark ink. The two legs must be in correct perspective.

When the ink strokes are dry, apply colour. It is better to use soft colours. The green on the plume can contain some warm tint. The shoulders and back can be painted with ink and ochre. Add dots in malachite and azurite on the neck.

Chicken

Ink plays an important role in representation of chickens. Display good brushwork and ink application in their depiction. Varying brushwork and ink are used in different parts. The feathers on the neck are tousled; the feathers in the tail are hard and dynamic. A short beak is preferable than a long one. Large feet are better than small ones.

Apply light colour. The crest is painted with cinnabar mixed with rouge. Press the brush tip to accentuate the fleshy value. The feet are painted with rattan yellow mixed with ochre and ink.

A white chicken can be outlined in light ink and coloured with light ochre before being painted with white. The colour should not be applied flatly. Do not let the white cover the ink. To paint a black and white chicken, white dots are applied before ink strokes are added. Chicks can be painted with ink dots before their eyes, beaks and legs are executed.

An artist can have a command of the various movements of chickens only through observation of life over a long time. Generally, the body can be executed before the head. But in certain occasion, the head can be executed first.

Duck

Paint the duck's head before its body. Place the head at different angles. Colours are applied after the ink strokes are dry. Its breast is painted with rouge mixed with ink.

A white duck can be outlined with light ink and painted with light ochre. White can be applied but do not let the white cover the ink lines. Shade the background to set off the white duck.

Sparrow and Chinese bulbul

Mix ochre with a little ink and paint the sparrow's head with a single dot stroke. Paint the back and wings with two ochre strokes. Before the strokes are dry, add ink dots.

The head of a bulbul can be outlined and painted with ochre and light ink. After the underpainting is dry, add a layer of azurite (label three).

Swallow and Kingfisher

Paint the swallow with dark ink. Before the ink is dry, add light ink strokes here and there so that the dark and light marks shade into each other.

The kingfisher is painted with ochre and ink and coloured with malachite, and occasionally, with a little azurite. Its breast is painted with the brush loaded with vermilion and a little carmine at the tip.

Wagtail

The wagtail is painted the same way as the kingfisher. The top of its head and belly is coloured with white.

Painting birds in ink: the silver eye

Painting birds in ink is a basic exercise.

The silver eye is also painted with ochre and ink, then coloured with malachite (label three) which should not be thick lest it should cover the ink strokes.

Painting Vegetables and Fruit

Chinese leaves

Contour the stalks with ink lines. Use broad ink strokes to depict the leaves. Wet-on-wet ink may be used. Before the ink strokes are dry, add veins to leaves with dark ink.

Radish

The white radishes are outlined in ink. Lift and press the brush to describe the shape. Red radishes can be depicted with broad strokes. Leave some areas blank.

Pumpkin

It is very important to present the pumpkin in proper perspective. The lines showing its structure help to bring out the feel of its mass. Use light ink dots to set off its tactile value. The dots should not be evenly added. The colour should not be applied flatly. Leave the highlight spots unpainted.

Grapes

To paint grapes you may use green or purple. Circle each grape with one touch. Attention must be paid to the spatial relationship between clusters. Add a dot to the outer side of each grape to display its direction.

Tomato

Tomatoes can be outlined or depicted with broad strokes, which must be applied in keeping with the structure of the fruit.

Pear, apple

Pears and apples can be outlined before colours are added. The stroke to display the stalk must be forceful.

Painting Insects

Anatomically all insects can be divided into three parts, the head, the back and breast, and the belly. Different insects are different only in size. Most insects have two antennas, two pairs of wings and six legs. Through observing nature and painting from life or by observing specimens, you can have a good understanding of the insect's anatomical structure and thus do a lifelike representation of them. Depicting insects in ink can be a daily practice.

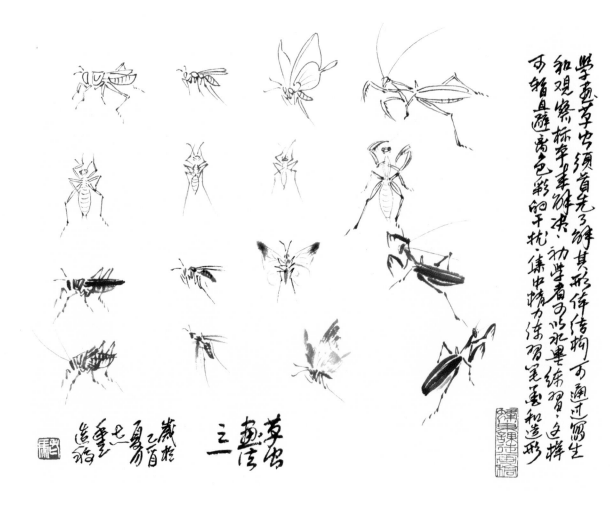

Butterfly, cicada, grasshopper and spider.

Strokes to show the legs are very important. Leave blanks at the joints. During the movement of the brush, pause sometimes to reinforce the brushwork. Vigorous and neat brushwork is preferable.

Beetles, mantis and katydid

Usually an insect is first executed in ink with "dotting" strokes, then coloured and detailed with strong colour strokes.

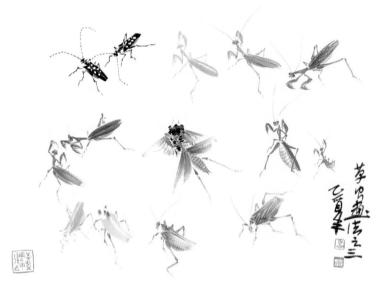

Dragonfly, wasp, water boatman

Pay attention to the relationship between insects and plants. Attention must be given to contrast of colours. If the flower is in warm colour, the insect should be in cool, and vice versa. A green dragonfly on a red lotus flower looks much more conspicuous than a red dragonfly on a red lotus flower.

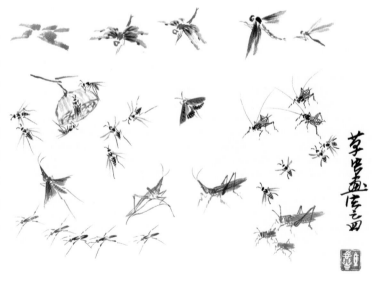

Composition

Composition deals with the arrangement of pictorial elements in a picture. There are special books on this topic. I recommend that the reader finds some books on composition. Rough guidelines are given here.

Asymmetry is a key word for Chinese composition.

— Chiang Yee, *Chinese Calligraphy*, Harvard University Press, 1972, p. 220

A key factor of good composition is the balance. The objects depicted in a painting should keep a balance but a symmetrical composition is not preferable. There are many ways to achieve balance in composition.

Unbalanced composition.

Balance achieved by adding a blade on the right. Yet the composition is not symmetrical. The leaf on the left is longer than the one on the right.

As a rule, arrangement of objects along a curved line is preferable to that along a straight line. S-formed composition is often used in Western painting. In Chinese painting it is used too.

Parrot by Ren Yi, Note the bough in a curved line as the main structure of the composition.

Taking off the flower on the left end of the bough, the composition is out of balance. The right half is too heavy.

An important principle of composition is "unity of opposites". To have a good composition the artist explores the relationship among opposite things such as large and small, long and short, high and low, square and round, simple and complicated objects, opposite colours such as bright and dark, strong and pale, warm and cool, opposite strokes such as dry and wet, fast and slow, as well as arrangement of opposite pictorial elements such as dense and sparse, fully exposed and partly hidden objects, and so on. To bring all these into a unity, the artist must put them into a balanced whole.

Birds by Hua Yan (1682-1756), note the birds look at each other, leading the viewer's sight from one to other, thus linking the whole painting into a whole.

Lotus by Zhang Xiong (1808-1886), the leaves in dark ink and the flower in white show contrast.

Flower by Ma Quan, created in 1712, note one flower is upward and the other downward.

Peacocks by unknown artist, note one peacock is fully exposed to the viewer while the other is half hidden behind the first one.

Peony by Zhao Zhiqian (1829-1884), note one flower is red and the other is white, the red flower is set off by green leaves and the white one is surrounded with ink leaves.

Peony by Hong Wu (19th century), note one flower is in full bloom and the other is in bud. The flower is the "host" and the bud, the "guest".

Peaches by Wu Changshuo, note the top of the painting has dense leaves and fruit balanced by the small cluster at the bottom, with space in between.

Plum Blossom by Jiang Tingxi (1669-1732), note the plum blossom is depicted with round strokes while the narcissus in the background is delineated with angular strokes.

Chinese artists often compare something in their painting as the "host" and other things as the "guests". They are responsive to each other. When more than two objects of the same kind appear in a picture, they should also be responsive to each other.

Pheasant and Hibiscus by Zhao Ji, note the bird's direction of sight follows the butterflies, bringing all objects in the painting into harmony.

Repetition is an often employed device to achieve coherence. For example, leaves of bamboo or in a grove are repeated representations.

Cold Brilliance in Autumn by Zou Yigui (1686-1772), note most leaves point to the lower left. The repetition of the same direction lends the picture coherence.

Well-deliberated empty spaces in a painting may be meaningful or evoking the viewer's imagination. In Chinese painting the sky and water as backdrops are often left blank, but the viewer still feels they are there.

Orchid by Wang Shishen (1686 — c.1762), note the large space on the right balances with the dense leaves on the left.

Composition of a painting must also fit the format of the painting. You cannot move the picture on a scroll to a fan without rearranging the composition.

Flower by Dong Gao (1740-1818).

Gallery

The peach is a symbol of longevity and hence used to extend the artist's good will for someone's birthday. Note the tip of one peach is straight and the other is oblique.

Three Thousand Years by Qi Baishi (1863-1957)

Spring Breeze by Wang Xuetao (1903-1982)

Narcissus by Wang Xuetao

Note the hair of the monkey is executed by using a split brush technique.

Spirit of the Wild by Zhang
Qiyi (b. 1915-1967)

Note the contrast between the two ducks. The one in the front is painted in dark ink and coloured while the one on the background is outlined in light ink.

Warm Spring Water by Xiao Lang
(b. 1917)

The banana leaves are painted with broad strokes while the quails are depicted with fine strokes. The bamboo branches at the right in front of the birds deepen the space in picture.

Banana by Sun Qifeng (b. 1920) and Ma Zhifeng

Black Swan by Ma Ming (b. 1954)

The swan is executed in meticulous mode. The red sun on the upper left provides a foil for the elegance of the swan. The large blank space is to be filled with the viewer's imagination.

Corn by Li Dongxu (b.1936)

Peacocks by Ma Zhifeng

Sisal by Ma Zhifeng

Night by Ma Zhifeng

Autumn Harvest by Ma Zhifeng

Magpies Over a Brook by Ma Zhifeng
and Li Yongping (b. 1950)

Peacock by Li Yongping and
Ma Zhifeng

Breeze by Zhang Tianxi (b. 1968)

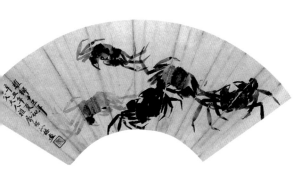

Crabs by Hu Qin 1908

Day Iris by Ma Zhifeng. Note the subdued tone.

Crabs by Ma Zhifeng

Peony by Ma Zhifeng
Note that in Chinese culture the peony is a symbol for wealth and rank

Chickens by Ma Zhifeng

Hawk by Wang Xuetao

Lotus by Ma Zhifeng

Birds and Flowers (a set of four scrolls) by Ma Zhifeng

Mountain Flowers by
Gong Wenzhen (b.
1945)

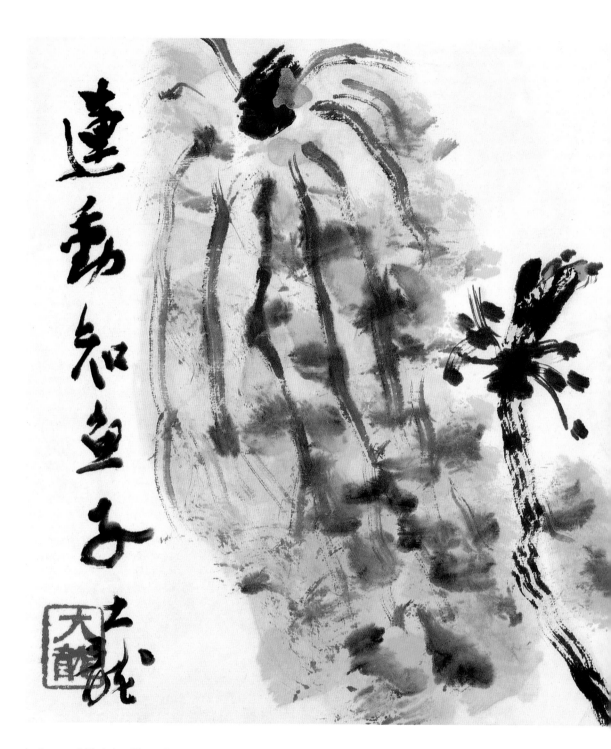

Lotus and Fish by Chen Dalong (b.1940)

Bamboo in Snow by
Zhang Lichen (b. 1939)

图书在版编目（CIP）数据

怎样画花鸟画 / 马志丰编著，温晋根编译
－北京: 外文出版社, 2007
（怎样做系列）
ISBN 978-7-119-04812-3

I. 怎… II. 马… III. 花鸟画—技法(美术) — 英文 IV. J212.27

中国版本图书馆 CIP 数据核字（2007）第 054216 号

责任编辑　温晋根
封面设计　蔡　荣
插图绘制　马志丰，温晋根，孙树明
策　　划　王贤春，李振国，肖晓明，温晋根

外文出版社网址:
http://www.flp.com.cn
外文出版社电子信箱:
info@flp.com.cn
sales@flp.com.cn

怎样画花鸟画

马志丰　著

*

© 外文出版社
外文出版社出版
（中国北京百万庄大街 24 号
邮政编码　100037)
北京雷杰印刷有限公司印刷
中国国际图书贸易总公司发行
（中国北京车公庄西路 35 号
北京邮政信箱第 399 号　邮政编码　100044)
2007 年(16 开)第 1 版
2007 年第 1 版第 1 次印刷
（英）
ISBN　978-7-119-04812-3
15000(平)
7-E-3759P